Mastering The Mental Side Of Tennis

Ernest Solivan

Mastering The Mental Side Of Tennis

ISBN: 978-0-6151-7356-6

Cover photo by Aries International
(U.B.T.O.)

In loving memory of Susan Solivan
1946 - 2014

"Though you're far away, I have only to close my eyes and you are back to stay. I just close my eyes, and the sadness that missing you brings soon is gone and this heart of mine sings."
Antonio Carlos Jobim

Mastering The Mental Side Of Tennis

Table Of Contents

Mastering The Mental Side Of Tennis

Table Of Contents

Introduction

Tennis originated in the monastic cloisters in northern France in the 12th century. However in the first few centuries in which it was played, the ball was then struck with the palm of the hand; hence, the name jeu de paume ("game of the palm"). It was not until the 16th century that rackets came into use, and the game began to be called "tennis." But, this isn't a book about the history of tennis, it is a book about the most neglected and least understood part of tennis, the mental part.

This is a book about HK and how you can use it to achieve peak performance as a tennis player by focusing on the mental part of your game. HK is a personal transformation technology that allows you to access, isolate and change undesirable mentally stored information preventing you from becoming a premier player.

HK's most salient characteristic is that it offers a very credible, rational and viable explanation as to why you experience performance problems during competition and offers a remedy that will allow you minimize and/or eliminate those uncharacteristic mental errors you experience preventing you from playing to the best of your ability during your matches.

There is an old saying that you cannot teach an old dog new tricks. This is a testament to how difficult change is for just about everyone. There are basically three elements necessary to create change in your life.

They are Sensation, Perception and Conception. Sensation is the capacity to experience; Perception is the capacity to be aware of what you are experiencing; and Conception is taking action to begin the process of change, or it can also represent rebirthing into a more positive experience.

I refer to HK as a language of change because it embodies all the elements necessary to facilitate and accelerate positive change in the athletes who experience it. HK does not diagnosis or label. Please respect the context in which I present this extraordinary and very effective discipline. It works on the simple premise that if it stresses you to play tennis, you are not going to do it well.

Please set aside your prejudices, beliefs and judgments and do your best to keep an open mind. HK is a little different and unusual twist on psychology. This discipline was created with the intention of allowing you to help yourself facilitate and accelerate positive changes that will immeasurably improve the quality of your life on the tennis court, as well as in your personal life. And, isn't that what we are all looking for?

There is a part of your being that houses everything you have ever learned about tennis. It is referred to as your Mind.

The Mind

When you set a goal to do something, one of two things will happen. You will either succeed or fail. What determines your success or failure is the information contained in your Mind. This stored information is the information you will use while attempting to accomplish your goal.

If the information in your Mind supports you in successfully completing your goal, the accomplishment of your goal will be easy and almost effortless. However, if the information in your Mind does not support you in successfully accomplishing your goal, the accomplishment of your goal will be very difficult and require a tremendous amount of effort.

Your Mind is generally thought to be the seat of consciousness. It is made up of every aspect of your being. There are many philosophies that view the Mind in a way that has created numerous fragments, i.e., the spiritual mind, the emotional mind, the etheric mind, etc. I found all these subdivisions of the Mind to be very confusing.

In HK I rely upon the very old axiomatic metaphysical concept known as "cause and effect." Several of the theories that support cause and effect are, "for every action there is an equal and opposite reaction;" "water seeks it own level;" and "what goes around, comes around."

Although I cannot see a tennis player's Mind, I can see the experiences that Mind is creating. For instance, if I am working with a tennis player who can't make it past the first round of a tournament, I must assume that he has information stored in his Mind to support him in doing that, or he would be doing something else.

It is important to note that your Mind supports you in everything you do. If you are struggling, your Mind is supporting you in struggling and it is doing so based upon information it has stored in its memory banks relating to success and failure. The tennis player's physical body is merely acting out (i.e., can't get past the first round) based upon this stored information, and it does it automatically.

To understand cause and effect, you must first understand that before anything physically happens in our lives, it must first start as a thought. So, if you want to change your undesirable experiences, you must change the thoughts in your Mind responsible for creating those undesirable experiences.

The goal of HK is to change the information in this player's Mind responsible for causing him to sabotage his success, and to do it as quickly as possible. Once he accomplishes that, his experience will change. When you change your thinking, you will change the experiences you are creating with those thoughts.

Before I explain how this is accomplished, it is important to establish a context and foundation whereby all the contributing factors to this failure phenomenon may be examined and understood. It is noteworthy to point out that in HK all we are dealing with is information.

Your Mind has basically two parts. The Conscious Mind, and the Subconscious Mind.

The Conscious Mind

The conscious mind is referred to as the "knower" because it has the ability to be aware of itself. It has the capacity to be aware of what it is thinking and feeling in the normal waking state. It also has the ability to know what it is doing and why.

One of the major functions of the conscious mind is its use of volition. Volition is defined as, "the act of using the will; exercise of the will as in deciding what to do; a conscious or deliberate decision of a choice thus made."

You are where you are in your tennis life right now as a direct result of the choices you have made using the volition contained in your conscious mind. It also provides us with short-term memory and can only focus on one thing at a time. This conscious mechanism uses the five senses sight, hearing, smell, taste and touch, to collect information which allows it to experience awareness.

The conscious mind uses this collected information to formulate your self-image, your prejudices, and your belief system. I believe that its most important function is that it allows us to set goals. The information collected by your conscious mind will influence the formulation of the goals you set throughout your life.

So, what happens when your conscious mind, using its volition, decides to engage in some particular activity like tennis? Well, it types out a memo of the instructions and sends it to another part of your mind known as your Subconscious Mind.

The Subconscious Mind

When you engage in a particular activity, like tennis, your conscious mind sends instructions to your subconscious mind, "Send me all the information you have relating to tennis." The information you access will dictate how well or poorly you perform.

If the information accessed from your subconscious mind is supportive, you will perform the activity easily and efficiently. However, if the information accessed is not supportive or contradicts the goal set by the conscious part, your activity will become very difficult and require a tremendous amount of effort.

Your subconscious mind is known as the "doer" because it merely does what it is programmed to do. Unlike the conscious part, it does not have the capacity to exercise volition, it merely "does."

Your subconscious mind acts out thorough the physical body and uses information it has stored in its memory banks relating to the particular activity. This "acting out" is done instantaneously and automatically. The information arrived into your subconscious mind through the conscious part's five senses (sight, hearing, smell, taste, and touch).

Your subconscious mind is a storage facility for all information that enters through conscious awareness. The one important feature to note about your subconscious mind is that when it is storing information it is impersonal. It doesn't say, "I am not going to store this experience because it was a bad experience." IT STORES EVERYTHING! It also provides us with long-term memory, and is the receptacle for your belief system.

Every forehand, backhand, volley, game, set and match you experienced is stored in your subconscious mind. Every win and loss was stored. Every emotional outburst was stored. Every time you broke your racquet in half was stored. Every shot you made and missed. Everything!

Your subconscious mind does not have a sense of humor, nor can it distinguish between a joke and something serious. Additionally, it cannot distinguish between something real or imagined.

Your subconscious mind can be likened to the hard drive of your computer with one notable exception. When using a computer, you have the option of saving or erasing the information on your screen. Every piece of information that enters the subconscious part is stored for future use. The conscious part will eventually use this subconsciously stored information when it engages in an activity that corresponds to the information in storage, like tennis.

The subconscious part will provide the conscious part with whatever information it has available. The information can be supportive as well as non-supportive. If there is one thing I would like you to get from reading this book it's that everything we do is subconscious. Do you remember years ago as a child when you were first learning to tie your shoes? At first it took a tremendous amount of time and effort. Now, you do it without thinking because it has become a subconscious act.

That is exactly what is happening with every other aspect of your life especially tennis. When you are on the tennis court you don't stop and ask yourself "What do I do now?" Everything is moving too quickly for your conscious mind to get involved and you are at the mercy of the information stored in the subconscious part.

This information will dramatically influence how you perform that day. That is, your physical body will "act out" based on whatever information is stored in your subconscious mind relating to tennis, and it is doing it below your level of conscious awareness.

In working with a young ATP player who had difficulty winning his matches, I asked him why he thought he wasn't winning his matches. He told me he gets nervous. When I asked him why he gets nervous he replied, "I don't know." That's because the reason for his nervousness is happening subconsciously, or below his level of conscious awareness.

I concluded he had a fear of losing, or perhaps a fear of winning. Consider this. Whatever points he accumulates as a result of the tournament he is now playing, he will have to defend those points next year. I instructed him to listen to my *Letting*

Go of Fear CD every day until he no longer felt nervous during his matches.

There is a very integral component of the mind that gets involved when the conscious and subconscious part interact. It is known as the Critical Factor.

The Critical Factor

After information enters your conscious mind, it is reviewed prior to storage in the subconscious part. The responsibility for this task belongs to a component of your mind known as the Critical Factor. The Critical Factor literally criticizes or reviews information that comes into conscious awareness. After its review, the Critical Factor must make a decision regarding the disposition of the information. The Critical Factor has two options. It can either store and act on the information, or reject it.

Everyone knows that the color of the sky is blue, but suppose I told you that the color of the sky was red. When that statement enters your conscious awareness, your Critical Factor will stop it momentarily and says something to the effect, "Let me check the information I have in subconscious storage relating to the color of the sky." The Critical Factor checks and discovers that the information in subconscious storage indicates that the color of the sky is blue. The Critical Factor proceeds to reject the statement, "The sky is red."

Getting back to the tour player who could not get past the first round of a tournament, his Critical Factor could not allow him to make it to the second round because the information stored in his subconscious mind contradicts the intentions of the conscious mind.

Whenever this player got close to making it to the next round, the conflict between his conscious mind and his subconscious mind would create so much stress in his body that he will start hitting his shots long or, start double faulting at crucial points in the match (Break point, set point, etc.).

His tennis game would literally fall apart. It's as if the Critical Factor goes on "red alert" and, using the player's physical body, proceeds to sabotage his efforts to make it to the next round. It is likened to what is referred to in physics as a quantum frenzy.

This quantum frenzy results from the conflict between the player's conscious and subconscious mind and creates chaos in the player's physical body which adversely affects the player's ground strokes, serve and every other part of his game.

You must understand that your Critical Factor is the part of your mind that tells you "You are not good enough to beat your opponent;" "You are not good enough to make it to the semi finals;" "You are not good enough to play professional tennis."

Imagine the Critical Factor as a guard, and that it is guarding all information coming into and leaving the player's mind. How do we change this information? How do we change this subconsciously stored information preventing you from playing your best during your matches?

In order to change subconsciously stored information, we must achieve Critical Factor Bypass.

Critical Factor Bypass

Critical Factor Bypass occurs when new information is allowed to bypass the Critical Factor of your mind in an effort to change subconsciously stored information. I will explain how HK can achieve Critical Factor Bypass in a later chapter.

Using HK to achieve Critical Factor Bypass allows us to accelerate change for the individuals who experience it. In order to more fully understand Critical Factor Bypass, we must first look to the advertising industry.

On many occasions advertising agencies will send sales copy to a psychologist, and ask, "Will this copy achieve Critical Factor Bypass for our product?" The ad agencies know that if they can achieve Critical Factor Bypass on anyone who hears or sees their commercials, their chances of selling their product or services are greatly enhanced. They carefully choose the people who star in these commercials, carefully choose the wording, and carefully choose the scenarios.

How can they motivate someone to buy their product or service? One way to do it is using fear. It cannot be done blatantly, it must be subtle. They accomplish this using authority figures. Have you ever noticed that in many commercials ad agencies will use policemen, judges, doctors, or firemen. All these professions represent authority figures and the ad agencies know that when a policeman tells you to do something, you normally do it without question. You do what you are told because the policeman was able to achieve Critical Factor Bypass.

Another very subtle tactic ad agencies will use to create Critical Factor Bypass is race and gender. I once saw a print ad that contained a Caucasian, an African-American, an Asian, an older gentleman, an older woman, a young man, and a young woman. They covered a lot of bases with that ad. And it was all done subjectively.

Sometimes the ad agencies will appeal to your emotions. I am certain you have seen the Michelin Tire commercial with a baby sitting in a tire. That commercial has been running for years. This particular commercial has been successful because the ad agency was able to achieve Critical Factor Bypass by using the baby to appeal to the emotions of the viewer. Babies are harmless, safe and sweet. Michelin must be selling a lot of tires, or they would not continue to use this very effective commercial.

Some of the other tactics used by ad agencies are humor and money. In fact, the next time you view or hear a commercial advertisement, ask yourself, "What are they doing in this commercial to achieve Critical Factor Bypass?"

We have examined the nuances of your conscious mind, subconscious mind, as well as your Critical Factor, and Critical Factor Bypass. Your mind must act out through the physical body and it does this using your brain.

The Brain

Although your mind is the decision maker, it is the brain's responsibility to carry out those instructions. The brain is a part of the Central Nervous System composed of approximately 10 billion nerve cells.

Each cell is linked to one another, and together they are responsible for the control of all functions in the physical body. The brain disseminates these instructions throughout the physical body using information provided by your mind in the form of electrical impulses.

The brain is an organ consisting of three major components. The Left Hemisphere, The Right Hemisphere and the Corpus Callosum. Although these three components are integral, they each have very specific and different functions, and can function independently should the need arise. The Left Hemisphere of the brain controls the right side of the physical body, while the Right Hemisphere controls the left side.

We need only look at a stroke victim to understand this phenomenon. Notice that in the majority of the cases only one side of the body is paralyzed. That's because the hemisphere of the brain on the opposite side of the affected area was so severely damaged during the stroke that it manifested as paralysis.

The corresponding side of the subject's physical body is not receiving electrical impulses (information) from the damaged hemisphere resulting in partial or total paralysis. There are degrees of this type of dysfunction between the brain and the physical body, and that total paralysis represents the extreme.

Since the Left and Right Hemispheres of the brain can function independently and have their own responsibilities, they need some way to communicate. This is accomplished using the Corpus Callosum. The Corpus Callosum is a band of nerve fibers that connect the Left and Right Hemispheres of the brain. The hemispheres share and exchange information (electrical impulses) that will eventually be disseminated to the physical body.

What I realized in my research in working with athletes was that the hemispheres of the brain have a tendency to "weaken" or "switch off." When one hemisphere is switched off, the opposite hemisphere will dominate. For instance, if your Left Hemisphere is switched off, your Right Hemisphere will dominate your activity. The hemispheres of the brain are continually influenced by and are reacting to, stimuli in their immediate external environment.

An excellent case in point occurred when I had worked with the Arizona State University men's golf team in 1991. The director of the golf program was observing one of the sessions with one of the team members on the driving range. He commented that the player was muscle testing weak for everything, as all the statements were relating to golf.

So I turned to the young man and asked him what his favorite school subject was. "Math," he replied. I then asked him to imagine himself doing Math. The young man muscle tested strong and both hemispheres of his brain were strong or switched on. Then I asked him to imagine himself playing in a golf tournament. The young man muscle tested weak, and both hemispheres of his brain were weak or switched off.

When he was doing Math, his physical body was relaxed, and both hemispheres of his brain were strong or switched on. The information he was accessing from his subconscious mind relating to Math supported him in doing it well and he excelled.

However, when he stepped on the golf course, it immediately created stress in his physical body, which weakened or switched off both hemispheres of his brain. Whatever he did on the golf course was a struggle. By the way, this player won his first collegiate golf tournament within thirty days after our session.

It doesn't matter whether the activity is golf, basketball, football or tennis. Every athlete has a brain with two hemispheres, and their brains function the same in tournament situations.

The brain does basically three things. It processes (learns), stores, and disseminates information. What kind of information? That would be any and all information relating to pictures, sounds, fragrances, culinary data, and touch. All three of the major components of the brain come into play when the brain is exercising these functions. Let's first examine the Left Hemisphere of the brain.

The Left Hemisphere

When the Left Hemisphere of the brain processes (learns) information, it only understands words, language and numbers. That's because the Left Hemisphere processes information sequentially, or one piece at a time.

The Left Hemisphere is one-dimensional, and can only focus on one thing at a time. The Left Hemisphere controls the right side of the physical body and it accomplishes this by sending information in the form of electrical impulses.

When the Left Hemisphere of the brain weakens or switches off, during the processing or learning stage, it's as if a bio-electrical short circuit occurs in your physical body, and the incoming information never reaches the hemisphere of the brain that is switched off.

Incoming information will only store in the hemisphere that is switched on. For instance, if your Right Hemisphere is switched off while your brain is learning, the incoming information will store in your Left Hemisphere.

Now, because there was no information, or very little, stored in your Right Hemisphere, when it's time for your brain to disseminate the information to you at some point in the future, you will only receive information from your Left Hemisphere. It's as if you are only getting half the information.

When the Left Hemisphere of the brain stores information, it will only store sequential information such as words, language and numbers. It will store information that is logical and organized. In other words, the information stored in the Left Hemisphere must be structured.

When the brain disseminates information to the physical body, the Left and Right Hemispheres deal with different and specific information. The Left Hemisphere of the brain provides the physical body with the following information and attributes:

Logic, action, decision making, critical, one-dimensional, mechanical, compulsive, doubt, cautious, judgmental, hard working, limitation, shame, rational, stoic, organization, reasoning, specificity, structure, boundaries, rules, rigidity, opinionated, intense, impersonal, cold, unfeeling, introverted, controlled, predictable, restricted, precise, serious, conservative, quiet, hard, intolerant, auditory, scientific, temporal (the now) arrogant, fearful and finite.

When you engage in an activity such as tennis and the Right Hemisphere of your brain is weak or switched off, your physical body is only receiving information, or a majority of the information, from your Left Hemisphere. This causes you to become left-brain dominant while you are engaged in tennis related activity. The result, you will exhibit one or more of the personality traits listed above.

For example, left-brain dominant individual's are very critical not only of others but of themselves as well. I am not intimating that these traits are necessarily bad, it's just that this abnormal brain dominance causes your behavior to become extreme. This phenomenon can create very dysfunctional experiences for the left-brain dominate individual both on and off the court.

Since our thoughts create our experiences, you can clearly see that many of us are only living up to half our true potential. Where is the other half of this information located? It is located in the Right Hemisphere of the brain.

The Right Hemisphere

When the Right Hemisphere of the brain processes information, it only understands movement and pictures. That's because the Right Hemisphere is spatial and can process information collectively rather than sequentially. This collectiveness allows it to process large amounts of information at one time. It will process information that has no structure.

For instance, if you were looking at a picture of a landscape with your Left Hemisphere, you would have to look at every piece of the picture individually because the Left Hemisphere processes information sequentially. You cannot see the whole picture if you are only looking at one piece.

The collective capabilities of the Right Hemisphere allows you to see the whole picture, while the Left Hemisphere provides you with the capacity to structure the collective information.

When we examine this phenomenon during the learning stage of our development, we can clearly see how the hemispheres of the brain influence how we learn. Let's look at an elementary school student named Harold. He is learning to read the sentence, "See Jack jump." If Harold had the Right Hemisphere of his brain weak or switched off while reading this sentence, his Left Hemisphere would dominate.

Now, keeping in mind that the Left Hemisphere processes information sequentially, Harold's Left Hemisphere will know and understand the words see, Jack, and jump. However, because Harold's Right Hemisphere is weak or switched off, he will have difficulty achieving total comprehension.

In order for that to occur Harold would have to send the information from his Left Hemisphere, via the corpus callosum, to the Right Hemisphere, and request additional information such as a visual of a boy jumping. With both hemispheres of his brain participating in the learning process, Harold will achieve total comprehension, no matter what he is learning.

Likewise, you can clearly see that abnormal brain dominance during the learning stages of your tennis game can have adverse effects that will stay with you for the duration of your career.

When the brain disseminates information to the physical body, the Right and Left Hemispheres deal with different and specific information. The Right Hemisphere of the brain provides the physical body with the following information and attributes:
Feelings, emotions, relaxation, beliefs, creativity, flexibility, physical movement, tolerance, visualization, artistic, spatial, self-esteem, forgiveness, unstructured, generalizations, procrastination, compassion, optimism, passive, funny, unreasonable, loud, expressive, foolish, passion, charming, humility, love, intuition, uncontrollable, multi-dimensional, imagination, addictions, laid back, open-minded, unorganized and infinite.

When the Left Hemisphere of your brain is weak or switched off, the Right Hemisphere will dominate your activities, from your decision making to your personality. Since your physical body is only receiving information from the Right Hemisphere of your brain, you will exhibit one or more of the above listed personality traits and attributes.

Think of the many times you observed someone who was frustrated and broke his tennis racket because of what was going on during a match. Or, how about John McEnroe? Do you think his Right Hemisphere was dominating his thinking during a match when he went into one of his tirades?

When your Left Hemisphere switches off during a match and your Right Hemisphere is switched on, look out, you are about to do some serious emoting. I believe McEnroe won a lot of his matches because his emotional outbursts adversely affected his opponents play. McEnroe was one of the best serve and volley players of all time. However, I sometimes wonder how McEnroe's career would have been affected if the Hawkeye electronic line devices have been in use back then?

The objective in HK is to switch on both hemispheres of your brain in relationship to a thought, statement or action. Having both hemispheres of your brain switched on insures that you will have access to information such as judgment, analysis and structure (Left Hemisphere), as well as creativity, imagination and intuition (Right Hemisphere). With both hemispheres of your brain providing you with information, you will experience total balance in your life, on and off the court.

A great analogy for explaining hemispheric balance is water. The Right Hemisphere can be likened to boiling hot water, while the Left Hemisphere is ice-cold water. By themselves, their temperatures are very uncomfortable. However, when you mix them together, you get a warm, comfortable and balanced temperature. When both hemispheres of your brain are switched on, you enter a mental space that athletes refer to as "The Zone."

Another salient difference between the hemispheres worthy of note is that the Left Hemisphere deals with "old" information, while the Right Hemisphere deals with "new" information. I once did a session with a tennis player and asked him to make a statement relating to winning the next tournament he had entered. When I checked his hemispheres using muscle testing, his Right Hemisphere was weak or switched off, while his Left Hemisphere was strong or switched on.

The results from the muscle testing told me he was approaching the goal of winning the tournament with his Left Hemisphere and that he was using "old" information. In other words, he was thinking "What did I do last week to win a tournament; what did I do last month to win a tournament; etc." Without the creativity provided by the Right Hemisphere of his brain, he will continue to use the old information creating the same result.

This may explain why some people seem to make the same mistakes over and over, or repeat the same behavior patterns throughout their lives in spite of their efforts to change. When you are "stuck" in your Left Hemisphere you will continue to use old information even though it didn't work last week or last month.

Without the new information provided by the Right Hemisphere in the form of creativity, it's as if you are walking through a mental revolving door. This new information augments and integrates with the old information allowing you to constructively handle whatever challenges you may be encountering during you matches.

There is another excellent analogy to contrast the hemispheres of the brain, and how they handle specific tasks. Let's assume that you have just purchased something that requires assembly. The Left Hemisphere of your brain will approach the task by saying something like, "Where are the instructions to this thing (?); I can't put this together without the directions!" Remember that because the Left Hemisphere is using old information, it is basically asking, "Show me the way some else did it, then I can do it."

Conversely, the Right Hemisphere will approach that same task by saying, "Hey, even if we don't have the instructions, let's try putting it together anyway." That's because the Right Hemisphere is providing your body with new information in the form of creativity, and will figure it out eventually.

The Right Hemisphere will risk (no instructions), while the Left Hemisphere will tend to play it safe (must have instructions).

If your left hemisphere is dominating your thinking during a match you will have a tendency to play it safe and stay back at the base line (Andre Agassi). If your right hemisphere is dominating your thinking during a match you will have a tendency to risk and come into the net (John McEnroe).

I am not intimating that left brain or right brain dominate players are necessarily bad, because if a left brain dominate player is playing a right brain dominate player, somebody's got to win the match. When both hemispheres are functioning we refer to the player as being "switched on."

What does a switched on player look like? I depends on the criteria. Before the open era you had player like Rod Laver who is the only player to win all four majors in the same year, and did it twice! Or, Don Budge who won six Grand Slam titles in a row from 1937 thru 1938. If you confine it to the open era, it would be who won the most tournaments during their career, or who won the most Grand Slam titles.

Most tournaments won list would go something like this: Jimmy Connors (109); Roger Federer (100); Ivan Lendl (94); Rafael Nadal (80); John McEnroe (77); and Novak Djokovic (73). Obviously Federer, Nadal and Djokovic aren't done yet.

If you use the Grand Slam criteria: Roger Federer (20); Rafael Nadal (17); Novak Djokovic (15); Pete Sampras (14); Roy Emerson (12); Rod Laver (11); and Bjorn Borg (11). Choosing the best player of all time is very subjective because if Federer, Nadal and Djokovic were playing with wood racquets would they have won as many Grand Slams? Food for thought.

When you can function on a tennis court with both hemispheres of your brain strong or switched on, you will achieve a level of play that most people just dream of. With access to structure, judgment and organization (Left Hemisphere), and creativity, intuition and imagination (Right Hemisphere), every decision you make on the tennis court supports you in playing your best and winning.

In HK it is imperative that we know what activity is taking place in the physical body in relationship to a statement, thought or action. This is accomplished using Muscle Testing.

Muscle Testing

There are three vital pieces of information necessary in HK in relationship to the subject matter which muscle testing allows me to obtain in relationship to a statement, thought or action. First, muscle testing allows me to determine whether the physical part of the body is weak or strong. Secondly, muscle testing allows me to determine the condition of the hemispheres of the brain. Thirdly, muscle testing allows me to post test and validate that the stress has been cleared from the physical body.

Muscle testing is a technique that has been widely used in the alternative health field for years and has been used in a variety of applications. I use muscle testing to determine whether stress is present in a player's physical body relating to a statement, thought or action. Since the physical body is merely acting out based upon information contained in the subconscious mind, muscle testing allows me to tap into that subconsciously stored information.

In his book "Switching On," Dr. Paul Dennison defines muscle testing as:

> *"Muscle testing is the art of isolating and testing one muscle at a time in order to determine if it is 'weak' or 'strong', relative to the strength of the individual being tested."*

There are forty-two muscle groups in the physical body. In HK, I muscle test the deltoid muscle. The deltoid is the larger triangular muscle of the shoulder, which raises the arm away from the side. If you held your right arm straight out from your side, parallel to the ground, and lifted your arm upward from that point, it is the deltoid muscle that allows you to execute that movement.

When I muscle test a player I will ask him to:

1. Stand with weight evenly distributed on both feet;
2. I have the player hold his left or right arm straight out or parallel to the ground;
3. I face the player standing in front of the outstretched arm;
4. I ask the player to look straight ahead and extend the fingers of his outstretched arm so that they are parallel to the ground;
5. I place my left hand on the player's left shoulder for support;
6. I place my right hand, using only two fingers (index and middle fingers) on top of the player's outstretched arm between the elbow and wrist;
7. The player is now ready to be muscle tested;
8. I will ask the player to resist upwards slightly, towards the sky, while I apply about 2 ounces of pressure downward towards the ground. This allows both the player and I to get a feel for the muscle test.

The key to muscle testing effectively is 2-2-2. Use two fingers, apply two ounces of pressure, and hold for two seconds. There are two possible responses to a muscle test. Strong or weak.

A strong muscle test indicates that my downward pressing motion was unable to budge the player's arm. A strong muscle test also indicates that there was no stress present in the player's physical body relating to the statement, thought or action for which I muscle tested.

A weak muscle test indicates that the player was unable to resist my downward pressure, and could not hold his arm parallel to the ground. A weak muscle test is evidence that stress was present in the player's physical body relating to the statement, thought or action for which I muscle tested.

What does a strong vs a weak muscle test tell me, if anything? Well, if I had had a player make the statement, "My goal is to win the U.S. Open," the strong muscle test signifies that the player's physical body would totally support him in the task. The absence of stress in the player's physical body indicates that there is information stored in his subconscious mind that would support him in winning the U.S. Open.

On the other hand, had the player muscle tested weak to the statement, the weak muscle test indicates the presence of stress relating to the statement. It basically stressed the player to say, "My goal is to win the U.S. Open." The weak muscle test tells me that the information stored in his subconscious mind would not support him.

A weak muscle test is the physical body's way of saying, "I am not doing that because I do not have information stored in my subconscious mind to support you, or that the information I have stored contradicts whatever it is you want to do."

The second piece of information I can obtain using muscle testing is the condition of the Right or Left Hemispheres of the brain in relationship to a statement, thought or action. For instance, when checking the condition of the Left Hemisphere, I would touch the left side of the head and muscle test. If I record a strong muscle test, the hemisphere is switched on. If I record a weak muscle test, the Left Hemisphere is switched off. I would do likewise to check the condition of the Right Hemisphere.

Checking the hemispheres of the brain allows me to determine how you would function while engaged in the activity for which we are muscle testing. For example, if I muscle tested you for earning $4,000,000.00 per year playing professional tennis, and you had your Left Hemisphere switched on and your Right Hemisphere switched off, your Left Hemisphere would dominate your approach to the goal.

You would exhibit the personality traits and attributes listed under the Left Hemisphere of the brain. The attainment of this goal might be a struggle for you because you would be lacking information such as intuition, creativity and imagination. Information provided by the Right Hemisphere of your brain.

Thirdly, and most importantly, muscle testing allows me to validate, through post testing, that the stress relating to the subject matter has been cleared from the player's physical body. Remember that your mind and physical body are integral. What affects one affects the other. In other words they mirror each other.

If I have you say "My goal is to win the U.S. Open," and you muscle test weak, and then have you say it again, and you muscle test strong, something obviously changed in your physical body and the way it reacted to the statement.

In HK, muscle testing allows me access to your subconscious mind. If subconsciously stored information is to be changed, it must be done subconsciously. Muscle testing allows me to inferentially (indirectly) access information from your subconscious mind using your physical body.

When your physical body is in a weakened state, it simply means that there is conflict between your mind and body. Your mind and body, as a result of this conflict, engages in a phenomenon known as "sabotage." Muscle testing allows me to interpret the language used by your physical body to communicate this sabotage state, and that language is Stress.

Stress

WHENEVER THERE IS CONFLICT BETWEEN YOUR CONSCIOUS MIND AND YOUR SUBCONSCIOUS MIND, IT WILL ALWAYS MANIFEST IN YOUR PHYSICAL BODY AS STRESS!

It's as if the conscious mind and subconscious mind are not on the same page. When stress is present in the physical body, it will always result in a weak muscle test and cause one or both hemispheres of the brain to weaken or switch off. The presence of stress creates a short circuit in the electrical system of the physical body and causes a biological fuse to blow.

It is crucial that you understand this phenomenon because it is at this juncture in the process that your physical body begins to sabotage your tennis game. When stress is present in your physical body, it goes on red alert because the information in your conscious mind does not match the information accessed from your subconscious mind. Your subconscious mind acting out through the physical part will do everything in its power to sabotage your success.

You must understand that your subconscious mind is not being vindictive. It is simply saying, "I do not have the information to support you in winning this match."

Taber's Cyclopedic Medical Dictionary defines stress as, *"...the result produced when a structure, system or organism is acted upon by forces that disrupt equilibrium or produce strain...the term denotes the physical and psychological forces that are experienced by individuals."*

Stress has an absolutely pervasive effect on the physical part of your physical body, and the prolonged presence of stress can manifest pathologically (disease).

When stress is present in your physical body, it creates a myriad of physiological changes. Some of the more salient physical reactions to stress are:

- Increase in the rate and force of heart beat;
- A rise in systolic blood pressure;
- Sweating of the palms and hands;
- Dilation of the pupils;
- Decreased digestion;
- Blood distribution from less to more active organs;
- Increased blood glucose (hyperglycemia);
- Etc.

Imagine trying to get your first serve in on championship point at a major tournament with all this going on in your body. When stress is present in your physical body, it interrupts the electrical signals from the brain to the muscles causing your physical body to weaken. It is when your physical body is in this weakened state that the sabotaging phenomenon occurs. You will either double fault on championship point, or hit an easy forehand volley into the net at a crucial point during the match. TV commentators will refer to these mental errors as nerves, but it is clear and simple stress.

This sabotaging phenomenon is so subtle that you will be totally unaware that you are doing it because it is all happening subjectively or subconsciously. That is to say that it is happening below your level of conscious awareness. All athletic movement, including the tennis serve, is subconscious in nature.

A tennis serve takes a matter of seconds. Remember that earlier we stated that one of the limitations imposed upon your conscious mind is that it can only focus on one thing at a time. The tennis serve is occurring too quickly for your conscious mind to be involved. Therefore, your physical body relying totally on the information contained in your subconscious mind in order to properly execute the movement.

It is important to note that there are different levels and degrees of stress that may manifest in your physical body ranging from very subtle to very severe. When a tour player executes his tennis serve it is impossible to see stress in his physical body with the naked eye. If he serves a double fault, there was definitely stress in his body.

However, since his subconscious mind stored that information, I can access that information later by merely asking him to remember the second serve he hit on match point that went into the net, and muscle test him.

Please remember that it is not what you are doing, but where you are doing it. Here's why. Take a 12" wide plank and connect it to two buildings five feet off the ground and ask someone to walk across it. No problem. Now, take that same 12" wide plank up to the 30th floor and ask that same person to walk across it. I guarantee you will get a different response. It is not what you are doing, but where you are doing it.

Are you playing in a major tournament or a 250 event? Are you serving at 15 all in the first set or, serving at break point to stay in the set. Your mind will access different information when you are playing the 100th ranked player in the world verses you playing the 2nd ranked player. And, it will dramatically influence the outcome of the match. However, I recently witnessed a top 10 player losing to a player ranked 116th in the world. Go figure.

What causes stress to manifest in the physical body besides walking on a 12" wide plank 30 stories high? Well, there is something that occurs while your subconscious mind is storing information, and it is responsible for causing stress in your physical body. This phenomenon creates what I refer to as Synthesizing Events.

Synthesizing Events

What we have learned up to this point is that the presence of stress in your physical body adversely affects you both physically and mentally. Physically, by weakening or switching off one or both sides of the physical body; and mentally, by weakening or switching off one or both hemispheres of the brain. When stress is present in your physical body, something is motivating it to manifest stress. That something is a “synthesizing event.”

A synthesizing event is created when emotions from a traumatic experience actually synthesizes (comes together) with the information as it is being stored in your subconscious mind. This synthesized information remains stored and dormant in your subconscious mind until your conscious mind engages in some activity relative to the information. Once your conscious mind accesses this synthesized information, it will manifest in your physical body as stress.

One of the best analogies I have ever heard in describing synthesizing events is to imagine that you have just purchased a brand new boat. The hull of this boat is clean and spotless. As time passes barnacles will attach themselves to the hull. The more barnacles that attach to the hull, the slower the boat will travel, until the boat accumulates so many barnacles it stops all together.

Synthesizing events are like barnacles that have attached themselves to the hulls of our lives. If you accumulate enough barnacles they may manifest physically as a nervous breakdown or chronic illness, or mentally as sabotaging everything you do. The barnacle analogy is likened to synthesizing events that players carry around with them from tournament to tournament. What's responsible for creating synthesizing events? Trauma.

Webster's defines trauma as, "1. A bodily injury or shock; 2. An emotional shock, often having lasting psychic effects." As you can clearly see, trauma can be experienced both physically and mentally, and can range from mild to severe. The physical trauma from an injury suffered during the final of a grand slam tournament causing you to withdraw, for example, will heal with time.

However, the mental (emotional/synthesizing event) trauma may remain locked in your mind and physical body for years unless you take some action to clear and release it. The intention of HK is to help players release trauma in the form of synthesizing events from their minds and bodies manifesting as performance stifling stress.

There are two types of synthesizing events. The "initial synthesizing event," and the "subsequent synthesizing event." The following analogy explains. Suppose you had a fear of heights. There was a first time you experienced that fear and it is referred to as the initial synthesizing event because it was the first time the synthesizing dynamics came into play relating to the experience.

That synthesized information is stored in the subconscious mind, and will remain dormant until you go near a high place again. Once this happens, the conscious mind sends instructions to the subconscious mind, "Send me all the information you have stored relating to being near a high place."

The subconsciously stored information from the first experience surfaces, and since an emotion has synthesized with the information, it surfaces as well. Your first reaction is, "Let's get away from this ledge!" The second experience created a subsequent synthesizing event.

Once you have left harm's way and are in a safe place, the initial synthesizing event is once again stored in the subconscious mind, and the subsequent synthesizing event is stored for the first time. Now you have two subconsciously stored pieces of information (or experiences) to support your fear of heights, and so on.

I can locate and access the initial synthesizing event relating to any subject using muscle testing because your physical body has stored and remembers every experience you have had. Imagine an onion. Its center represents the kind of tennis player you would like to become. Over the years you have accumulated layers of synthesizing events preventing you from realizing that potential.

These synthesizing events are responsible for creating the problems you are now experiencing with your athletic performance, and if you don't get rid of them you will carry them with you from match to match. In order to access the center of your onion (your true potential), the layers of synthesizing events must be peeled away, and that is exactly what HK and this program will help you do.

It is my belief that 95% of all synthesizing events are stored in your subconscious mind during a period in your childhood development known as the Egocentric Stage.

The Egocentric Stage

There is a period in your childhood known as the egocentric stage, and it occurs between conception and 7 to 8 years of age. It was during this stage in your development when most of the synthesizing events were stored in your subconscious mind.

Webster's defines egocentricity as, *"Regarding the self or the individual as the center of all things; Having little or no regard for interests or feelings other than one's own; Self-centered."* The egocentric child is so self-centered that the first thought they have when something goes wrong in their lives is, "What did I do wrong?"

If you ask a three-year-old boy if he has a brother, he will answer yes. If you ask that same three-year-old boy if his brother has a brother, he will answer no. That's because the egocentric child cannot objectify his experience, he can only experience.

It's as if he cannot see himself. The reason for this phenomenon is that the egocentric child's mind does not possess a critical factor. Remember that the critical factor allows the mind to accept or reject incoming information passing through the conscious mind.

Without the capacity to criticize incoming information, the subconscious mind of the egocentric child stores everything! At age 7 or 8 the child's critical factor starts kicking in. During the child's teen years, it is operating at full capacity because teenagers know everything and adults know nothing.

After the teen years our criticalness starts reversing and by middle age most of us experience a softening of our attitudes and come to realize that criticism was all a waste of good energy to begin with.

The absence of the critical factor also denies the egocentric child the capacity to rationalize. You cannot rationalize with someone who is incapable of objectifying his experiences. Some of the other anomalies associated with the egocentric child:

* Absolutize – You either love me or you hate me;
* Personalize - Takes everything personally;
* Idealize their role models – If dad says I'm stupid, it must be true;
* Self-blame – What did I do wrong;
* Shame – There must be something wrong with me;

Children have very limited resources when dealing with trauma. The only way they know how to deal with trauma is to block it out. They accomplish this by switching off one or both hemispheres of their brains depending on the severity of the trauma. This switching off will influence their behavior and the decisions they make for the rest of their lives.

In the 1980's John Bradshaw brought to light information relating to dysfunctional families. In a dysfunctional family, the members are simply not getting their needs met. But, what kind of a family environment would produce a functional child or adult? The following quote is from a book titled Trauma and Recovery by Dr. Judith Herman:

"The developing child's positive sense of self depends upon a caretaker's benign use of power. When a parent, who is so much more powerful than a child, nevertheless shows some regard for that child's individuality and dignity, that child feels valued and respected; he develops self-esteem. He also develops autonomy, that is, a sense of his own separateness within a relationship. He learns to control and regulate his own bodily functions and to form and express his own point of view."

Wouldn't it have been nice to have been raised in this environment? The truth is that 99% of all families are dysfunctional. This dysfunction leaves most children who experience it filled with shame and doubt. Dr. Herman continues:

"Shame is a response to helplessness, the violation of bodily integrity, and the indignity suffered in the eyes of another person. Doubt reflects the inability to maintain one's own separate point of view while remaining in connection with others. In the aftermath of traumatic events, survivors doubt both others and themselves."

The switching off anomaly doesn't make children who experience it functional, it makes them <u>more</u> functional, relatively speaking. Also, it is during this stage in our development that we accepted beliefs about ourselves that simply were not true. We accept beliefs that we were not tall enough, good enough, thin enough, smart enough, this enough or that enough.

If a child is shown respect, he learns to respect himself and others. Disrespecting a child traumatizes him. Children believe that they are perfect until they hear otherwise. They are so incredibly vulnerable during this stage of their development.

Many children, who eventually turn pro, started learning their tennis skills during this very sensitive stage of their development. Whatever they learn, good or bad, will follow them the rest of their careers.

Here is an extraordinary example of how things we learn about ourselves during the egocentric stage of our development stay with us the rest of our lives.

One day a teacher asked her students to list the names of the other students in the room on two sheets of paper, leaving a space between each name. Then she told them to think of the nicest thing they could say about each of their classmates and write it down. It took the remainder of the class period to finish their assignment, and as the students left the room, each one handed in the papers.

That Saturday, the teacher wrote down the name of each student on a separate sheet of paper, and listed what everyone else had said about that individual. On Monday she gave each student his or her list. Before long, the entire class was smiling. 'Really?' she heard whispered. "I never knew that I meant anything to anyone!" and, "I didn't know others liked me so much," were most of the comments.

No one ever mentioned those papers in class again. She never knew if the students discussed them after class or with their parents, but it didn't matter. The exercise had accomplished its purpose. The students were happy with themselves and one another. That group of students moved on.

Several years later, one of the students was killed in Viet Nam and his teacher attended the funeral of that special student. She had never seen a serviceman in a military coffin before. He looked so handsome, so mature. The church was packed with his friends. One by one those who loved him took a last walk by the coffin. The teacher was the last one to bless the coffin.

As she stood there, one of the soldiers who acted as pallbearer came up to her. "Were you Mark's math teacher?" he asked. She nodded, "Yes." Then he said, "Mark talked about you a lot." After the funeral, most of Mark's former classmates went together to a luncheon. Mark's mother and father were there, obviously waiting to speak with his teacher. "We want to show you something," his father said, taking a wallet out of his pocket. "They found this on Mark when he was killed. We thought you might recognize it."

Opening the billfold, he carefully removed two worn pieces of notebook paper that had obviously been taped, folded and refolded many times. The teacher knew without looking that the papers were the ones on which she had listed all the good things each of Mark's classmates had said about him. 'Thank you so much for doing that," Mark's mother said, "'As you can see, Mark treasured it."

All of Mark's former classmates started to gather around. Charlie smiled rather sheepishly and said, "I still have my list. It's in the top drawer of my desk at home." Chuck's wife said, "Chuck asked me to put his in our wedding album." "I have mine too," Marilyn said, "It's in my diary." Then Vicki, another classmate, reached into her pocketbook, took out her wallet and showed her worn and frazzled list to the group. "I carry this with me at all times," Vicki said and without batting an eyelash, she continued, "I think we all saved our lists."

If you tell a 6 year old his isn't good enough, he has no way of stopping that information. It goes right into storage and will be used at some point in his future to create his self-image. If you treat that same 6 year old with respect he will learn to respect himself and others, and he will carry it with him for the rest of his life.

For all you tennis teachers and coaches out there, I entreat you to be ever so mindful of what you say and do to children during this very fragile and incredibly vulnerable stage in their development.

Sometimes the trauma is so severe that it causes both hemispheres of the brain to weaken or switch off. This creates a condition known as Dissociation.

Dissociation

Children do not have a lot of options when dealing with trauma. They deal with it by blocking it out. They accomplish this by switching off one of both hemispheres of their brains depending upon the severity of the trauma. When both hemispheres of the brain switch off it creates a condition known as "dissociation."

Dissociation occurs when specific mental functions become separated (or dissociated) from the mainstream of consciousness and, as a consequence, are lost to the individual's awareness and voluntary control.

When a tennis player, for instance, dissociates during a tournament while executing his serve, he cannot feel (Right Hemisphere switched off), nor is there structure to his serve or mental processes (Left Hemisphere switched off).

I did a session recently with a young player, and asked him to imagine himself playing during the first round of the U.S. Open. When I muscle tested, and checked the hemispheres of his brain, they were both switched off. He was experiencing dissociation, and with both hemispheres switched off it's as if the player's body doesn't have access to information provided by the brain. In this mental state his exit from the tournament would be quick.

It's the 3rd set tie breaker of the 1981 U.S. Open between Tracy Austin and Martina Navratilova. Up to this point Navratilova has served 11 double faults. A very frustrated Navratilova had pushed an easy volley wide to set up championship point and was down 6-1 in the third set tiebreaker before missing her first serve. Navratilova proceeded to blast her second serve into the net for her 13th and final double fault of the match. Austin wins 1-6 7-6 (7-4) 7-6 (7-1).

If you dissociate during a match, you couldn't get your first serve in if your life depended on it. You will miss a simple volley that you had made hundreds of times during practice. In effect, your tennis game is "switched off."

There is a way to help you keep both hemispheres of your brain switched on during competition. This is accomplished with the use of the HK Performance Trigger.

The HK Performance Trigger

We now know that when a tennis player experiences a traumatic encounter, the emotions from that trauma will synthesize with the information stored in his subconscious mind and adversely affect his future performances. In order to clear the synthesizing event, a desynthesis must occur. In order to reverse this phenomenon, I employ the HK Performance Trigger.

The HK Performance Trigger is used to release and/or neutralize the trauma and all associated emotions connected to that trauma from your subconscious mind manifesting as stress in your physical part. In other words, the intention of the HK Performance Trigger is to sever the emotional trauma from the information stored in your subconscious mind creating the stress. It works because *"energy follows intention."*

The more you do something the better you get at it. So, the more you use the HK Performance Trigger, the stronger and more effective it becomes. In HK, trauma, synthesizing events and mental baggage are all synonyms and are imprinted in your subconscious mind. The HK Performance Trigger was designed to help you neutralize the psychophysical anomalies responsible for your problems on the tennis court.

This program, utilizing the HK Performance Trigger, is designed to help you play your best to win the tournament; and to help you peel the onion and become a top 10 player. The remainder of this book will show you how to program in the HK

Performance Trigger, and how to use this program so that you may gain the maximum benefit.

Tennis Mechanics

Earlier I had mentioned that when there is stress present in your physical body, it would cause one or both hemispheres of your brain to weaken or switch off. This switching off phenomenon not only affects your thought processes during your matches, but also can adversely affect your tennis mechanics.

When stress is present in your physical body it causes it to weaken. It is when your physical body is in this weakened state that you will double fault on match point and wind up losing the match, or hit a seemingly easy volley into the net at a crucial point in the match.

The presence of stress will actually cause one or both hemispheres of your brain to weaken or switch off. This is the anomaly responsible for adversely altering your tennis mechanics. Here's why.

The Right Hemisphere of your brain controls the left side of your physical body, while the Left Hemisphere of your brain controls the right side. When your Right Hemisphere weakens or switches off during your tennis stroke, it weakens the left side of your physical body. When you hit your ground stroke with a weak left side, it dramatically alters the mechanical dynamics of your stroke and will cause you to hit an errant shot.

This may occur at a crucial point during the match. Did you ever notice that sometimes a player has set point and double faults. However, when he gets to the deuce court, he hits an ace. Back at the ad court, he hits a simple volley into the net. This may go on for 3 or 4 times before he closes out the set.

The reason? When he is at the deuce court he has both hemispheres switched on, and that allows him to hit his ace. When he gets to the ad court his left or right hemisphere switches off or he dissociates, and hits an errant shot. It is at "crunch time" when stress will manifest for the player. If a player can remain calm and relaxed during these crunch times, both hemispheres of his brain will remain switched on, and he will close out the set or match.

There is no way you can hit any of your tennis shots consistently with your physical body in this weakened state. This weakened state is so subtle it cannot be seen with the naked eye, and that is where muscle testing comes in.

This switching off phenomenon not only affects you physically, but mentally as well. For instance, if you are in your left hemisphere when playing a match, you will have a tendency to stay back and not come into the net because the left hemisphere of your brain will play it safe, while your right hemisphere will risk coming into the net and getting passed. You can see how this switching off will clearly affect the decisions you make during your matches.

With both hemispheres switched on you will intuitively know when to stay back and when to come into the net. How many times have you seen a match go 7-6 in the first set, and think, "Man, this is going to be a good match," only to see the final score 7-6, 6-2, 6-1. It's as if the losing player just mentally collapsed and had the wind knocked out of his sails.

All the players on the professional tennis circuits know how to correctly execute ground strokes, volleys, serves, etc. The one thing that separates them all is what's going on in the five inch space between their ears during crunch time.

This program is specifically designed to give you a resource. A resource to help you become as mentally prepared for your match as you can possibly become so that you may use that space between your ears to help you play your best to win.

In HK, I employ the HK Performance Trigger to help you keep both hemispheres of your brain switched on during competition. What you are about to learn in the following pages will help you remain calm, focused and relaxed during your matches and help provide you with mental clarity so that the decisions you make on the court support you in doing your best to win your match. You will be shown step by step:

1. How to program in the HK Performance Trigger;
2. How to use the HK Performance Trigger before, during and after your matches;

3. How to use the "Mind Mastery For Tennis" program;
4. How to use the HK Performance trigger during your practice sessions;
5. How to conduct HK Journaling after each match so that you don't carry mental baggage with you into your next match, or tournament;

Let's first show you how to program in the HK Performance Trigger.

Programming In The HK Performance Trigger

There are three steps to programming in the HK Performance Trigger:

Step #1: Read the following statement aloud:

"I, (state your name), now accept and integrate into my mind and body the HK Performance Trigger which is stating, thinking or hearing the word 'relax' and touching the thumb and index fingers of both hands, to immediately and permanently neutralize and remove all initial and subsequent synthesizing events, and all trauma manifesting as stress in every cell, organ and tissue in my physical body, and to 'switch on' both hemispheres of my brain, and to activate that part of my mind that supports and allows me to experience more wealth, health, happiness, peace, joy, prosperity, safety and security in my life, and all other attributes I may require to help me experience the lifestyle of my choosing, to help me successfully accomplish all my goals, and to improve the quality of my life relating to every statement, thought and action I experience, layers one through infinity, and to help me maintain a mental state that will enhance my ability to win every game, set, match and tournament in which I compete and I will never do anything to interfere with my mind and physical body's ability to win. This or something better."

Step #2: Say or think the word "relax" and touch the thumb and index fingers of both hands, then release and open your fingers.

Step #3: Read the statement in Step #1 again. Remember to read it aloud so that you involve as many of your senses as possible. The HK Performance Trigger, which is stating or thinking the word "relax" and touching the thumb and index fingers of both hands, is now programmed into your subconscious mind.

The HK Performance Trigger is intended to help you stay calm and relaxed during your matches, and most importantly during your tennis strokes. If you can remain relaxed when you execute the various tennis shots during a match, both hemispheres of your brain will remain switched on. This insures that both sides of your body remain strong allowing the proper execution of your ground strokes, serve, etc.

It will also provide you with the mental clarity to help you create a strategy that will support you in playing your best. This ultimately results in more consistent play and dramatically enhances your chances of winning your match.

Remember, when you are calm and relaxed that is when both hemispheres of your brain function at maximum capacity, and it will allow you to play your best during the match.

The HK Performance Trigger is designed to help you:

- To instantly, automatically and permanently release all trauma from your conscious and subconscious mind manifesting as stress in your physical body;

- To instantly, automatically and permanently switch on and strengthen both hemispheres of your brain relating to every statement, thought or action you experience no matter what the activity;
- Neutralize and remove from your mind and body whatever is stopping you from playing your best during your matches;
- To stay focused and relaxed during your matches;
- To do your best to win whatever tournament you may be playing;

There is an excellent process we use in HK to extract information from your subconscious mind. It is called HK Journaling.

HK Journaling

One of the limitations of your conscious mind is that it can only focus on one thing at a time. If you are having problems with your tennis game, there is usually more than one thing responsible for those problems. The HK Journaling exercise allows you to bring up those problems, or the negative experiences you had during your match, one at a time in order of their priority.

HK Journaling entails the use of open-ended statements to access subconsciously stored information manifesting as problems during your matches. Grab a pencil and a blank piece of paper and draw a line down the center of the page. At the top of the left side of the page write the word Negative. At the top of the right side of the page write the word Positive.

Using open-ended statements list the negative things that occurred for you during your match on the left side of the page. For instance, let's assume that you have just completed the first round of a tournament, and you lost 7-5, 3-6, 2-6. Here is how you would document this information.

1. One of the negative things that occurred during my first round match was: I had difficulty getting my first serve in;
2. The second negative thing that occurred during my first round match was: I had 21 unforced errors.
3. The third negative thing that occurred during my first round match: Etc.

After you have finished documenting all the negative things that occurred for you during your match, go to the top of the right side of the page and document all the positive things that occurred for you during your match.

1. One of the positive things that occurred during my first round match was: I won the first set;
2. The second positive thing that occurred during my first round match was: I only double faulted twice;
3. The third positive thing that occurred during my first round match was: Etc.

It is important to also focus on the positive things that occurred during your match because if you only focus on the negative that is all you will see. It reminds me of an old saying I once heard, "You are never as good as you think you are, but you are never as bad either." Looking at both negative and positive elements of your game just gives you a more balanced perspective on what's really going on for you.

As you can clearly see, the HK Journaling exercise allows you to document a tremendous amount of information regarding your match, and the problems that came up for you. It is especially important for you do this exercise after losing a match. Doing the HK Journaling exercise after a loss will be a good indicator whether or not you can remain objective while doing this program. Please do your best.

Now, let's discuss how the HK Performance Trigger is used to clear the information that surfaced for you during your post match evaluation.

How To Use The HK Performance Trigger

With the onion analogy I explained that the center of the onion represents the type of player you have the potential to become. The layers of synthesizing events that have settled in your subconscious mind are preventing you from becoming that player.

What's creating problems with your tennis game right now is the fact that you carry these synthesizing events with you from match to match, and from tournament to tournament. It's as if you are walking through a mental revolving door.

I suggest that you do the HK Journaling exercise at the conclusion of each and every match and at the conclusion of each and every tournament in which you compete. What follows is a four step process that will allow you to peel away the layers of synthesizing events responsible for creating the problems you are now experiencing with your tennis game:

<u>Step #1:</u> If you haven't already, go back to the chapter on Programming In the HK Performance Trigger. Program in the trigger by following Steps 1 through 3 (Once the trigger is programmed in you never have to do it again);

<u>Step #2:</u> Read your HK Journaling list starting with the negative things that came up for you during your match or tournament, and read them one at a time;

<u>Step #3:</u> After reading the first item on the negative side of your list, hit your trigger. Say or

mentally state the word "relax" and touch the thumb and index fingers of both your hands, and open them. Move to the second negative thing and repeat the process until you have gone through the entire negative list;

Step #4: Now, move to the positive list and repeat Step #3 until you have gone through the entire positive list;

Here's why this is so effective. Suppose that one of the negative things that came up for you during your match was that you had difficulty getting your first serve in. When you read this sentence, your conscious mind will send instructions to your subconscious mind, "Send me all the stored information you have relating to why I had difficulty getting my first serve in."

When that information surfaces within your physical body, it will no doubt have a synthesizing event connected to it. When you hit your HK Performance Trigger, it allows you to neutralize and remove it. Why? Because that is the intention of the trigger and energy follows intention.

It helps you peel another layer from this onion that has grown around your tennis game. The more layers you can peel off, the closer you will get to the center which contains your ability to become a top 10 player.

My suggestion is to punch holes in the completed pages and keep them in a three ring binder. Once a month or so, review them and see if you can find any patterns that may be developing in your game that need addressing. In fact, the question you should be asking yourself after each match is, "What could I have done to have improved my play during this match?"

If after hitting your HK Trigger you take a deep breath or yawn, it simply means that a shift in your energy field has occurred. You are in effect "peeling the onion."

You will spend countless hours working on your mechanics during practice. How much time to do spend working on the mental part of your game? Spend an hour after a match before you go to bed, and do this process. I guarantee you it will pay dividends.

The HK Performance Trigger can also be used during your practice sessions and during your matches as a Pre-Point Routine.

The Pre-Point Routine

You will be integrating this pre-point routine into your tennis game for one reason and one reason only, to help you become as calm and relaxed as possible during the execution of your serve and ground strokes.

When you are relaxed during your serve and ground strokes it allows you to keep both hemispheres of your brain switched on which keeps both sides of your physical body strong allowing you to mechanically execute your strokes with consistency and continuity.

Here's how you do the pre-point routine before a game:

1. Before you serve or receive, mentally state your goal for the game (i.e., my goal is to win this game);
2. Mentally state the word "relax" and proceed to play the game;

Here's how you use the pre-point routine for your serve:

1. Just prior to hitting your serve, mentally state your goal for the serve (i.e., flat serve down the middle, etc.);
2. Mentally state the word "relax" and proceed to hit your serve;
3. If a second serve is required, mentally state your goal for your second serve;
4. Mentally state the word "relax" and proceed to hit your second serve;

There are many reasons why this pre-point routine is so effective. The most important reason is that it allows you to remain focused on your whole purpose for being out there, and that is to win. It also allows you to set a goal for each point, and the continued use of the HK Performance Trigger "relax" will help you remain relaxed and forget about that easy forehand volley you missed on the last point.

Another excellent advantage in using this pre-point routine is a phenomenon known as "compounding." Compounding occurs when the same suggestion is layered upon itself many times. The incessant use of the word relax will eventually condition your mind and body to relax.

When your body is relaxed during competition you will achieve peak performance. Your play will become much more consistent, and you may even begin to enjoy the experience.

Using The HK Trigger Between Points

Although I encourage post match evaluations, the HK Trigger can also be used between points and games to do a quick mini evaluation of the point or game you have just played. The intention of this procedure is to prevent you from carrying synthesizing events created by a double fault from one point or game to the next.

For example, let's say that you have just completed a long rally and you hit your forehand into the net to end the point. As you are preparing to serve or receive, ask yourself, "Why did I hit that ground stroke into the net?" Then mentally state the word relax. This allows you to neutralize the mental anomaly from your mind and body responsible for causing you to hit that errant shot.

Here's why this is so effective. When you asked the question about your errant shot, your conscious mind sends instructions to your subconscious mind, "Send me all the information you have in storage relating to the shot I just hit into the net?"

When that information surfaces from your subconscious mind it will not doubt be accompanied by a synthesizing event. When you hit your HK Trigger, it allows you to neutralize and remove yet another layer of this onion that has grown around your tennis game.

Remember that it has taken you years to create this onion, and that you have been carrying around this mental baggage for years. Continued use of the HK Trigger will help to accelerate the removal of these layers of synthesizing events from your mind and body responsible for your marginal play during matches.

The physical body never does anything arbitrarily. If you miss a shot that causes you to lose an important game, set or match, something in your mind motivated you to do that. During the change over, do a quick mini evaluation of the two games you have just completed for any anomalies that may have surfaced for you during those games.

Use your HK Performance Trigger to neutralize those anomalies. This prevents you from carrying the synthesizing event responsible for you missing that important shot into your next game. It simply allow you to put it behind you.

Setting Goals

After Tiger Woods won his first Masters, he skipped a tournament, and came back and won the next tournament. During his post tournament interview he was asked why he thought he won the tournament. Tiger Woods looked at the interviewer with a surprised look and replied, "Because it was my goal to win it."

How does your physical body know what your mind expects from it if you do not set a goal? Set a goal for each point, match and tournament. Even if your physical body sabotages your efforts when you set a goal, at least give it the benefit of the doubt. ALWAYS SET A GOAL TO WIN!!!

You are setting a goal for each point when you use your pre-point routine. Here's what you do to set a goal for each match and each tournament. The night before the tournament, grab a pencil and paper and write your goal for the tournament. Read your goal aloud the night before the first round of each tournament.

Example:

Step #1: I, player's name, now choose to win the XYZ Tournament, and I will do my best to win this tournament by winning every match I play no matter who my opponent is, and I will remain calm, relaxed and focused and I will never do anything to interfere with the successful completion of my goal to win. This or something better;

Step #2: Hit your HK Performance Trigger by stating or thinking the word relax and touching the thumb and index fingers of both hands, and opening them;

Step #3: Read your goal aloud again.

The night before you first match, and all subsequent matches, grab a pencil and paper and write your goal for the match. To set a goal for each match do the following:

Step #1: I, player's name, now choose to win my match against, opponent's name, and I will do my best to win by outplaying my opponent, and I will remain calm, relaxed and focused and I will never do anything to interfere with the successful completion of my goal to win. This or something better.

Step #2: Hit your HK Performance Trigger by stating or thinking the word relax and touching the thumb and index fingers of both hands, and opening them;

Step #3: Read your goal aloud again.

Anytime you do something different your body sends up a red flag and says something like, "What a minute, nobody sent me a memo, what are you doing?" If you are not accustomed to setting goals, the first several times you do it your mind and body may ignore or sabotage your efforts.

When you do set a goal to win a tournament one of two things will happen. You will either have the worst tournament you have had in 5 years, or you will win it. That's because when you set a goal to do something that is when your "stuff" (synthesizing events) comes up. The "stuff" is that part of you that thinks you are not good enough. It must be cleared out, and that is what HK is intended to do.

If you set a goal to win a match and don't, it simply means your onion needs additional peeling. Do your best to remain objective (neutral) and ALWAYS SET A GOAL BEFORE EACH POINT, MATCH AND TOURNAMENT TO WIN!

Using Your Imagination During Practice

I recently saw a short segment on the Tennis Channel where Richard Williams was telling one of the Williams sisters, when they were children, to image that they were serving championship point at the US Open. Between the two, they have won eight US Open titles and countless others. (Please note that this was implanted in their minds during the egocentric stage of their development.)

Imagination is defined as, *"The action or faculty of forming mental images or concepts of what is not actually present to the senses."* When you imagine yourself doing something you are going to subconsciously access the same information as if you were physically doing it. Using your imagination during your practice sessions has a twofold benefit.

First, since your imagination is located in the right hemisphere of your brain, every time you use it you are exercising that part of your brain. If you can keep the right hemisphere of your brain switched on during your practice sessions, chances are you will keep it switched on during your tournament matches.

Secondly, your subconscious mind cannot distinguish between something real or imagined. Using imagination in conjunction with the HK Performance Trigger allows you to neutralize any mental blockages you may have subconsciously stored relating to a particular tournament situation.

Think of the most stressful situation you normally encounter during tournament play, and mentally imagine yourself in that situation during your practice sessions. For instance, imagine that you are playing in the final of the United States Open and you are serving for the match against the number one player in the world. See if you can get your first serve in. If you miss it, ask yourself, “why did I miss my first serve on that point?”

Then hit your HK Performance Trigger by mentally stating or thinking the word relax. Keep creating that situation until you get your first serve in. Then move on to other stressful situations you encounter during your matches and repeat the same procedure.

Here is a game, set and match point exercise you can do. During your practice session before a match, imagine serving against your next opponent on the deuce court. Mentally state, "game point" and hit your serve. If you miss your spot, mentally state, "Why did I miss my spot on game point?" Then hit your trigger. Keep hitting your serve until you hit your spot. Do the same for set point and match point. Move to the ad court and repeat.

When you are playing your match with your next opponent, on game point your subconscious mind will say, "Been there and done that." Remember your subconscious mind cannot distinguish between something real or imagined. If you don't believe me try telling someone who has a fear of heights that they have nothing to be afraid of.

Mentally creating stressful tournament situations during practice will immeasurably help you cope with those same situations during actual tournament play.

Does imagination work in other sports? During the final round of the 1994 United States Women's Open Golf Championships, Lauri Merten was on the putting green, before the start of her round, imagining herself putting to win the tournament. Four hours later she was hoisting the trophy as the 1994 United States Women's Golf Open Champion. Imagination is a very powerful and effective tool, and it works. I entreat you to religiously integrate it into your practice regime.

Mind Mastery For Tennis

I created a program for tennis players called *Mind Mastery For Tennis*. It includes the DVD titled *Change Your Thinking, Change Your Life*, and a 30 minute CD titled *Winning At Tennis*. The DVD will explain how we use muscle testing in HK and has a segment that will show you how to muscle test yourself.

The CD *Winning At Tennis* is designed to work on a subconscious level because that is where you performance problems are located. At the beginning of the CD I have programmed in the HK Performance Trigger (relax). The CD contains over 100 statements relating to tennis and winning. Each statement is followed by the trigger word relax, and can be used by tournament as well as recreational players.

Listening to the CD before your match helps you mentally prepare for your match by clearing your mind and body and puts you in a mental state that will allow you to play your best.

Listening to the CD after your match helps to peel away the layers of mental anomalies from your mind and body that came up for you during your match. If you are not playing to the best of your ability, it simply means that your "stuff" came up during your match. This stuff, in the form of synthesizing events, is responsible for the problems you experienced during your match.

If you have been playing in tennis tournaments for 10 years, you have 10 years worth of information stored in your subconscious mind. If some of that information was stored as synthesizing events, they were put there in layers over this 10 year period.

Repeated listening to the CD helps to peel away these layers of synthesizing events from your mind and body and puts you on the road to becoming the player you would like to become. It literally changes the subconsciously stored information you have accumulated over the years relating to your tennis game.

Remember, when you are out there standing on Center Court of the United States Open your conscious mind will send instructions to your subconscious mind, "Send me all the information you have in storage relating to playing in the United States Open." The information you access will dictate how well or poorly you will perform.

If you experience a really horrible match, that's when you really need to listen to the CD. Please do your best to remain objective. I recommend that you listen to the *Winning At Tennis* CD every day for the first 30 days (If you have any matches during this time frame, listen to the CD one to two hours before your match).

After 30 days, listen to the CD one to two hours before each match, and before you go out to practice, and the evening after you match or practice. Listening to the CD before your match gives you a pre-game mental preparation regime that will help put you in a mental space that will allow you to play your best.

Listening to the CD after your match allows you to clear any synthesizing events that came up for you during your match so that you don't carry them into the next round of the tournament. You can also buy a small portable CD player and place it on the headboard of you bed.

Turn it on before you drift off to sleep with the volume low and hit the repeat button. You will derive the same benefits listening to the CD in this manner because although you may not consciously hear it, you are subconsciously hearing it. You may also listen to the CD driving in your car; jogging; etc.

I cannot adequately stress the significance of listening to the CD every day you touch a racquet. Even when you practice you are accessing information from your subconscious mind relating to your tennis game. Some of the information you access during your practice sessions will have synthesizing events attached to them, and they must be neutralized or you will carry them into your next match or tournament.

Conclusion

I don't know what you are going to have to do to become the kind of tennis player you would like to become, but on some level of your awareness you do. The stress present in your mind and body during your matches is actually blocking you from obtaining that information. Doing this program faithfully will help peel away those blockages preventing you from realizing your true potential to become a top 10 player.

To gain the maximum benefit from this program it is important to use the entire program which entails:

- Programming in the HK Performance Trigger;
- Using your HK Performance Trigger along with your imagination during your practice sessions;
- Using your pre-point routine before each point;
- Setting goals before each match and tournament;
- Performing mini evaluations during the change overs and using your HK Performance Trigger;
- Faithfully doing your post tournament evaluations using the HK Journaling exercise;
- Religiously listening to the CD *Winning At Tennis.*

My heart really goes out to professional tennis players who play in front of tens of thousands, and sometimes millions of TV viewers. It reminds me of the movie As Good As It Gets. There is a scene where Jack Nicholson is telling Greg Kinnear that he wants to get romantically involved with Helen Hunt. Greg tells Jack, "Go ahead, tell her how you feel about her. The one thing you have going for you is your willingness to humiliate yourself."

A wise man wrote years ago that we can't be Batman to all the Robins in the world. You cannot control what others think or feel about you, but you can control what you think and feel about yourself. And, believe me that will be a full time job.

It is said that adversity introduces a man to himself. I trust that the next time you encounter adversity on or off the tennis court that you will remain objective enough to understand where it came from and how to constructively deal with it. Remember that tennis, like life, is relative, and that among the blind, the one eyed man is King. "Relax"

****

Other HK programs available at
www.hk-relax.com & Amazon.com:

Mind Mastery For Golf
Mind Mastery For Soccer
Mind Mastery For Money
Mind Mastery For Tennis
Mind Mastery For Hitting
Mind Mastery For Learning
Mind Mastery For Pitching
Mind Mastery For Coaching
Mind Mastery For Basketball
Mind Mastery For Winning
Mind Mastery For Selling
Mind Mastery For Peace
Mind Mastery For Learning
Mind Mastery For Weight Loss
Change Your Thinking Change Your Life (DVD)

Other books by Ernest Solivan:

Mastering The Mental Side of Soccer
Mastering The Mental Side of Tennis
Mastering The Mental Side of Hitting
Mastering The Mental Side of Winning
Mastering The Mental Side of Football
Mastering The Mental Side of Pitching
Mastering The Mental Side of Coaching
Mastering The Mental Side of Basketball
Mastering The Mental Side of Putting
Existential Psychophysics (HK Book)
When The Wheels Fly Off (Golf Book)
Pro Se Cites & Authorities

For more information about Hemispheric Kinesiology
contact:
Performance Consultants International
Website: www.hk-relax.com

www.ingramcontent.com/pod-product-compliance
Lightning Source LLC
LaVergne TN
LVHW091153080426
835509LV00006B/664
* 9 7 8 0 6 1 5 1 7 3 5 6 6 *